BEAT THE BULLY

A Guide To Dealing With Adult Bullying

1st Edition Published in 2011

Book Formatted & printed by Lulu.com

Copyright of Alex Gadd

ISBN - 978-0-9559899-1-9

ACKNOWLEDGEMENTS

It would be wrong of me to write this guide on dealing with bullies without mentioning some of the people for whom I am grateful for in helping me complete this book. The first person who I would like to share my gratitude for is Adam Wiseman who helped me in designing the cover to this book. Art, especially by the computer is something which is beyond me and as such, I am grateful for Adam for designing the delightful cover to this book. My designs would certainly not have been anywhere near as good.

I would also like to give acknowledgements to both my parents who spent the time spell checking and proof reading this manuscript, correcting my various errors, on which there would had been many. Also I would further like to give my gratitude for their support and encouragement in this book for without it, the chances are you probably wouldn't be reading it.

I would also like to give special thanks to my brother Chris as well, whose advice throughout the years on how to deal with bullies, be it as a child or adult, has worked its way somewhere into this book. I don't think I would of being able to written this manuscript if it weren't for the advice he had given me over the years on how to stand up to bullies.

Finally, I would like to give special appreciation to all those people who have stood by my side and helped me when it comes to dealing with bullies, especially the grown up ones. People who have helped in this area include friends of mine at my social club (and few friends at my former social club).

There are also many other people who have enabled me in their own way to be able to write this book, if reading this, you will probably know who you are!

CONTENTS

INTRODUCTION

If I were to ask you to imagine what a typical bully looks like, what sort of images do you conjure up in your mind? If like most people, you'd probably imagine something along the lines of a typical school bully, be it;

- The boy who pushes his fellow classmates around and threatens others with violence to get what he wants (like Nelson Muntz from 'The Simpsons')
- The girl who spread gossip about you behind your back and openly mocks you with her shallow friends (like one of the girls from the movie 'Mean Girls').

Fortunately within the UK, attitudes towards bullying within the school system have changed quite somewhat, mainly in that it is not at all tolerated and those caught bullying others will be punished. This has changed quite somewhat compared to a generation ago when bullying within schools was often seen as natural part of growing up and vital part of character building.

Unfortunately like the rest of us, bullies also grow up and become adults. While it is true that many people who were bullies as children happen to grow out of this behaviour, a great number don't (and a few people even become bullies as adults). Furthermore, many adult-based organisations, be it work, social, political or even charitable unfortunately don't like to admit that they have bullies within their ranks. As such, on hearing from one of their members that they are being bullied by another, instead of trying to solve the problem, the organisation would rather sweep the problem under the carpet.

Recently I was listening to a radio program on bullying in the workplace. What I found very interesting about this program was the fact that one of the people who called into the program claimed to work quite high up in the Human Resources (HR) department for a large company; though he didn't say which one for fear of losing his job. Yet what he said was of most interest, mainly that the purpose of HR isn't to protect the rights of the employee (that is down to the unions) but instead its purpose is to protect the rights of the company. Hence if you are being bullied and have reported it to the HR department, expecting them to fix the problem with your interests at heart, than you may be in for a nasty shock. The same can also be said for other types of organisations as well.

Worse still, many people who are being picked on by a bully don't even know that they are being targeted and as such, suffer the psychological pains that those who are bullied go through, without truly knowing the cause of these reactions. So if you believe that as you are not being bullied, this book isn't really for you, than think again. You just might not realise that you are the target of a bully.

Likewise, there are also some people who are the polar opposite, always run to management claiming to be bullied by someone when it most obviously clear that the person they are referring to isn't really a bully but naturally just a difficult or unpleasant person. Maybe you know someone like this? Naturally these people don't tend to be regarded very highly by management or anyone else in the organisation.

So if you believe that you are being bullied (or not) and feel powerless because you don't know what to do, then help is at hand. In 'Beat The Bully, A Guide To Dealing With Adult Bullying' you will uncover a very simple method of reflection which you can apply to anyone you know to work out whether you are being bullied by them or not (though I'd recommend using it only on those who make you feel unpleasant to be around rather than everybody you know as you would probably end up a bit paranoid).

You'll also learn;

- Some of the more common myths behind bullying, such as 'Bullying is just a personality conflict' as well as how these myths are wrong and how it really is

- How despite bullies coming in all different shapes and sizes, most bullies can be categorised as either one or a mixture of the following categories; physical bully, verbal bully and passive bully

- A list of some of the psychological effects that bullying has on a person, including lowering of self-esteem and confidence

- If you are being bullied, what you can do to minimize the psychological effects of the bullying and get yourself back into clearer state of mind

- The action steps that you can take to stop the bully and his campaign of intimidation against you, without raising your own fists and even if your organisation happens to be reluctant to do anything

Lastly I would like to add that throughout this book, you may notice that I do not at any time refer to the target of a bully as a victim. The reason for this is because unlike many other books on bullying, I don't think it is right to label a person who is being bullied as a victim. The reason for this is because I think calling someone a victim is a bit derogatory. Instead I believe a better label would be 'Target' for as the name suggests, a target is someone who is being targeted by a bully.

So as an adult, if you find yourself at mercy of a bully within an organisation, be it work, social, etc and feel that you are powerless to do anything, than read on for help is at hand!

WHY ME?

Are You the Victim of a Bully?

It is part of the human condition to want connect with others and in return, have your efforts reciprocated in kind and in an ideal world, this would be the case. From the moment we are born, we all want to feel loved and cared for. Unfortunately not too long after we leave the crib, we quickly learn that not everyone returns the friendship we show them. Or perhaps the bit of friendship they do give back is peppered with nastiness, where we are left feeling disempowered within ourselves and confused as to if this person really is our friend or not.

Even worse, some of the acquaintances we meet along the journey of life will seem to carry out a campaign of hatred towards us. These people are what I would classify as a 'Bully.' Although the term bully tends to be used quite loosely, my definition of a bully is;

'anyone who leaves you feeling worse off on an overall basis, whether by active means such as belittling you, intimidating you, (both physically or verbally) etc, or by passive means such as either repeatedly ignoring or dismissing you, giving you more work than most with least praise, etc'

It is worth noting that in the above definition, I have put 'etc' at the end of both active and passive methods of bullying, the reason for this been that there are thousands if not millions of different methods to which bullies use to try and intimidate you. To try and list all these methods would require an encyclopaedia sized book which would become out of date very quickly due to new bullying tactics being deployed all the time.

If you are feeling slightly daunted by the sheer number of bullying tactics out there, than it may be of comfort to know that all of these tactics can be dealt with using the same few techniques (as outlined in chapter 6. I haven't come across a bullying tactic yet which is beyond at least one of the techniques outlined in this chapter, whether the bullying method is verbal, physical or cyber (that's right, bullying is now happening online as well)!

So how can you tell if you are being bullied, with all the various methods that these folk seem to employ to get at you? Well the bad news is that you can't detect all bullying because some of it happens so subtlety that you probably don't even know it is happening. For example, the newsagent who is always mildly unpleasant to you when in his shop but friendly to his other customers can be said to be a bully. Yet unless you were watching his interactions with his fellow customers 24/7, you'd probably never even realise he was picking you out. Or the person who spreads rumours about you behind your back, which you unfortunately never get to hear of.

FACT

Many people who claim never to have been the target of a bully probably have been but are either ashamed to admit it for some reason or simply not sensitive enough to know that they were in fact being bullied!

The good news however is that our minds (despite not being able to detect all bullies) are highly attuned to detect threats to our well-being and a bully is certainly a threat to ones well-being. Yet in the cases where you are undecided as to whether you are being bullied or not, simply ask yourself the following questions

1. Do many of the interactions that I have with (name of person) leave me feeling somewhat negative i.e. stressed, anxious?
2. Does (name of person) seem to have the same affect (or similar) affect most of the people around him as well?

Now if your answer to the question one was no, than the person in question most probably isn't a bully (well not one who is much of a threat to your quality of life). Yet if the answer was yes to question one and yes to question two, than the person isn't probably a bully in that he is not picking on you. He (or she) is probably one life's unfortunate few who is unpleasant to most people. Yet if your answer was both a yes to question one and two, than you most certainly do have a bully on your hands.

If so, do take comfort in the knowledge that the bullying in question is certainly nothing to do with you personally. From personal experience, (indeed, even I have being bullied and to read up more about my personal experiences of bullying, refer to chapter 5) in times of being bullied it can seem very personal, like you are the reason for the bullying, whether it is because of who you are. **NOTHING COULD BE FURTHER FROM THE TRUTH!** Bullies bully for one reason alone. The reason for this is (drumroll)

'they have some inadequacy within their characters, be it from the fact that they only have a small character, else because they have some emotional or neurological dysfunction'

Either way, please note that you (the target) are not in any way intentionally the issue and nothing much you could have done could really change that. Bullies choose their targets because of an almost infinite number of different reasons, ranging from the way you speak reminding them of unpleasant person in their past to the fact that you happened to do something which they perceived as a weakness and they could latch onto. Either way, the reason for the bullying lies solely with the bully, never with you the target.

Yet despite not being accountable or able to control the reasons why a bully has picked you out, take note that **you are responsible with how you go about dealing with the bully and the bullying**. You as a conscious person with free will have the ability to choose your attitude to the bullying and how you will respond to the bullying. If you can take only two things away with you from reading this book, may it be these two things;

1. You are not accountable for the bullying or why he has picked you out
2. You are able to choose your attitude to the bullying and how you will respond to the it

Before moving on to explain the most common types of bullies, I would like to further reassure you (if you are being bullied) with the knowledge that not only is the bullying NOT personal but that you are almost certainly not the only target of the bully. You read correctly, most bullies don't only pick on one person but usually have several targets on the go at the same time. Come to think of it, this may also be one of the reasons why bullies don't want you informing others about what is going on, in case you and another target happen to meet up. To bully one person at a time is easy, but two or three people at a time, more difficult.

Remember, bullies are cowards and as such, don't like the prospect of been beaten or even challenged, especially by two of their targets standing up as a united front!

For Marion, today was going to be the first day of her new life. Having recently graduated from university and spent few months looking for work, she was about to step into her first proper job, the first day of her career. As a high achiever and active socialiser in school and university, she assumed that she would very easily fit into the office job she had applied for. People loved her, as did teachers and former employers (from part-time work she did to help her through university).

Actually, her first day didn't go to badly, her charm rubbed off on most people, she pretty much learnt where everything was. In itself, the day was a 9/10, would have been a 10/10 if it weren't for Rebecca, the middle-aged woman whose desk was diagonally across from hers. Not that Rebecca was nasty or anything, just cold and non-communicative with her, despite being friendly with everyone else. Trying to be the optimist though, Marion simply brushed it aside as 'you can't win everyone.'

Unfortunately over the coming week, the problem didn't seem to remain with Rebecca, as more and more people began to treat her coldly, no longer openly talking with her when they did beforehand. And after a few weeks, Marion quickly found herself in an unpleasant situation, where nobody was willing to talk to her anymore, except the few 'unpopular ones' in the office, the nerds who nobody wanted to talk to. As she had stupidly not bothered to make the effort to make friends with them, (choosing to hang around the more popular people) there wasn't much communication between them either.

Disappointed by the change of opinion of her, Marion decided that it didn't matter too much, as long as she focused on doing a good job and impressing her bosses; she had friends outside of work who she could hang out with. Though she would admit that her confidence had taken her battering, she was determined that she would weather this storm.

Unfortunately this wasn't to be the case, when it appeared certain co-workers were deliberately not passing on the details of important meetings, etc. Hence the meeting would take place and she would get in trouble by her manager for not being there. Not wanting to make further enemies, Marion didn't want to mention that the person who was forwarding the memo around the office didn't include her (and that it was happening quite a few times).

So the first few months for Marion had turned from what was meant to have been a bright new chapter in her life to a living nightmare, with nobody talking to her and her manager starting to think that she was incompetent. Fortunately, help was to come and from the most unusual of places. George, one of the 'unpopular types' approached her when on one of her lonely lunch breaks and informed Sue as to what was really going on. He informed her how the office really has two bosses, the official boss and Rebecca, the unofficial boss whom with clique of friends, had built up a subculture where, she ruled.

Marion almost felt sick on hearing how Rebecca had apparently taken a dislike to her, seeing Marion's confidence and charm as a challenge to her authority and as such, had ordered her small gang of followers to make Marion as unwelcome as possible. From what George told her, Marion learnt how that Rebecca and co were spreading all sorts of rumours about her to others in the office, such as she used to be a prostitute, was a home-wrecker and even that she hung out with unsavoury characters outside of work.

On asking George why he was informing her of all this, Pete said that he and some others who were also the targets of Rebecca's bullying and that they were building up a case to take to the company HR, the company head office and if need be, the newspapers. He then went on to say how they had noticed how Marion was also the target of Rebecca's hate campaigns and if she would be willing to act as a witness to this, to which Marion gladly agreed. Before heading off back to their desks, George added how for now, it would be best if Marion didn't say anything about this to Rebecca, adding how the element of surprise is what is best. Marion agreed.

That afternoon was tough, as working so close to Rebecca, part of Marion wanted to go up to her and give her a piece of her mind, but she remembered George's advice. Yet at the same time, Marion no longer felt so alone and powerless, she now knew that there were others in the office that she could go to for support. Also, she knew that with such a determined group of targets, Rebecca's days were numbered!

TYPES OF BULLIES

WHY THERE ARE MORE CATERGORIES OF BULLIES OTHER THAN MALE & FEMALE

As part of the marvelousness of life, we humans are all unique; there are literally no two humans who are the same. Even identical twins have their slight differences. Unfortunately this variety also means that there isn't one set standard to a bully. Bullies all differ slightly from one another, hence making it impossible to categorise simply by external looks or attitudes to life whether he or she is a bully. Or to use the identical twin example, one twin could be the most decent person you could ever hope to meet, the other a bully.

Yet despite the uniqueness among bully-boys and bully-girls, there does tend to be certain styles of intimidation and aggression which bullies tend to adopt. In this chapter, I will reveal to you some of the more common styles of bullying which bullies employ and the tactics of bullying which these styles *tend to* use. Please note the reason for putting the words 'tend to' in italics is because these are only common bullying styles. As bullies are all human with their own individuality, many of the bullies in the world would tend to be a cross of two or more of the styles, if not a unique style in their own right.

WARNING
PLEASE DO NOT ASSUME THAT JUST BECAUSE A BULLY WHOM YOU MAY HAVE IDENTIFIED FROM THE PREVIOUS CHAPTER DOESN'T FIT INTO ANY OF THE STYLES BELOW, DOES NOT MEAN HE IS NOT A BULLY!

PHYSICAL BULLIES

A physical bully is basically a bully who tends to get physical or threatens his targets with the prospect that he will get physical with them if they do not comply to his demands. Unfortunately it seems to be mostly male bullies who fall into this category due to the fact that as a species, the males tend to be more violent and aggressive than the females. Yet don't get me wrong, there some female bullies out there who also fall into this category.

I'm sure that there are times in your life when you have encountered a physical bully, whether their aggression is aimed directly at you or someone else at the time of your encounter. Often the aggression or the image they are trying to project is so violent that many people would naturally feel afraid to stand up to the bully or help someone else confronted by the bully (though I must add that seeing someone being bullied physically or mentally, and doing nothing, not even reporting it, means that you are an enabler to the bully).

Though they do exist, it is rare to find someone who is just a physical bully and not also any other type of bully. A purely physical bully would be the type of person who picks his targets and automatically starts a physical fight (or threatens physical action) without any verbal contact, etc. beforehand. Many physical bullies however, (before becoming such bullies) start off as;

VERBAL BULLIES

A verbal bully is a bully who rather than using his fists, prefers to bully with his mouth, whether directly at you or by spreading gossip about you behind your back. In my experience, these are by far the most common types of bullies, usually only becoming physical bullies in the extreme cases.

A pure verbal bully can come in many different forms. One type of verbal bully is what I nickname 'The Blitzer' for whenever they see one of their targets, they simply blitz that target with nasty comments, whether it be bitchy, belittling or just plain rude. Out of the different types of verbal bullies, this type is the easiest to spot for their actions are plain to the world to see; there is usually very little façade behind their acts, such as 'I was only joking.' Usually though, these sorts of bullies tend to rely on an audience of those around. It is like they want to be a stand-up comedian, you the material and everyone else the audience, cheering and laughing while you break-down.

Please note that when in the presence of a Blitzer, it is very easy to think that everyone in the room is on their side, simply because of the fact that everyone else is either standing back and not helping or worse yet, laughing and joining in like a comedy sidekick to the Blitzer. The reason for this is because Blitzers when in their bullying mode tend to project an aura of dominance and friendliness over most others in the room. This aura tends to be picked up by others around as 'I am your friend, join me, but beware that if you don't, I can just as easily turn on you as well!' This is why many others (who are insensitive or just plain weak in their own right) will tend to join it.

Another type of verbal bully is what I nickname 'The Stealth Attacker.' Unlike the Blitzer who will go in guns blazing, rallying troops whilst they go along, the Stealth Attacker is the complete opposite. These people don't want an audience; very often they don't even want others in the room to know that you are their target. As the name suggests, the Stealth Attacker is one who attacks you in stealth like manner. Such a manner includes;

- Spreading unfounded gossip behind your back
- Have a dig at you when nobody is about
- Say odd nasty comment to you in public, intentionally knowing that you will read the comment the true way while everybody else would read it another way

A prime example of the double-meaning comment I heard recently was one female acquaintance saying to another female friend of mine (in ear-shot of myself and a few others) 'us two larger ladies could certainly do with xxx plan.' Initially I thought the comment was just a bit insensitive (but genuine in that the attacker did also add herself into it; though I couldn't honestly see why my friend needed to lose weight) but only later did I find out she was a bully and that this was a Stealth Attack on my friend.

Another type of bully which I have personally witnessed (as I'm sure you have many times throughout your life) is the Manipulator. The Manipulator is one who takes delight in pressing your buttons, trying to manipulate you to always feel guilty, anxious or stressed. Yet what makes the Verbal Manipulator Bully different from your average Manipulator is that the former usually picks out a few targets and continuously focuses all his manipulative efforts on those people. It should also be said that these Manipulators aren't necessary Stealth Attackers or Blitzer's but can be both, either saying manipulative comments when no one else is around or intentionally in front of a large audience.

PASSIVE BULLIES

It sounds like a contradiction in terms, a Passive Bully but don't be fooled, these people do exist but in my opinion, are the hardest to stop for they are not really attacking you so to speak. Instead of going out of their way to intimidate or belittle you, Passive Bullies tend to use the passive bullying strategies which I mentioned in the previous chapter on the definition of bullying. These being ignoring you except for when they absolutely have to, giving you more work than most others (if in the position to) with no praise.

It is due to Passive bullies using these strategies that it becomes hard to actually catch the bully, at the very least find a way to define their bullying as many times because their behaviour really borders on the edge of bullying behaviour and well, not bullying-behaviour. I mean though it may hurt you to hear this, people do have the right to not like you (or me). As such, it is perfectly in their right to be cold to us or simply ignore us when they can. I suppose in a working environment, the only real way you can catch a passive bully out is if they exceedingly push you too far with overwork and no praise or constantly dismiss your views. Yet even then, it is tricky to truly catch them out as the passive bully can easily deny this is really taking place.

To most people, Gill was a happy, out-going type of person. She would stop and speak to almost everyone at her work, be it those who were above her in the organisation to those whom were right at the bottom of her workplace, even the cleaners who were perceived by most others working in the company as an untouchable. Everyone saw Gill as a delight, a positive upbeat woman who would stop and ask you how you were doing and be genuinely interested in what you said.

Yet note how she almost speaks to everyone. Unfortunately for a few, Gill didn't seem to take any interest in them whatsoever or even note their existence and Helen was one of those people. Helen, a fellow co-worker of Gill's never got a hello, good-bye, etc from Gill. On the few times Helen approached Gill and tried to open a friendly dialogue, Gill simply gave brief answers to Helen's questions, refusing to carry on the conversation, finally informing Helen that she has work to get on with.

Yet Gill wasn't always like this to Helen. On first starting work at the company, Helen remembers Gill initially being friendly to her but after a few days, Gill just went cold to

Helen for no reason. On questioning Gill as to her sudden coldness, Gill informed Helen that she was acting no differently to her then she was to anybody else. Yet to Helen, this was certainly not the case.

Naturally this made Helen feel bad about herself, feeling angry for being treated in such a way whilst guilty as well; what could she said or done to offend Gill so much, and why does Gill deny that there is a problem.

Due to the on-going overwhelming emotions in regards to the situation, Helen decided to approach her boss and asked if she could be moved to another desk away from Gill and her overly happy attitude to others.

Please remember, if you are a target of a bully, this doesn't necessarily mean that they will fit the mould of any above styles, so don't assume that you are not being bullied because your bully doesn't exactly fit one of the above types. Bullies come in all shapes and sizes, like their targets. Also it is worth remembering that a bully is anyone whose interactions overall leave you feeling negative while treating most other people differently.

Yet above all else, take knowledge in the fact that despite their various sizes and methods of attack, bullies are all the same inside, that being **Cowards to the core**

THE DAMAGING EFFECTS OF BULLYING WITHIN & WITHOUT

HOW BULLYING AFFECTS ONE

Very often when the topic of bullying is brought up in a conversation, it still surprises me how many people believe that bullying is nothing more than a personality clash; a conflict between two (or more) people. Unfortunately nothing could really be further from the truth for while a personality clash implies two strong-willed people trying to get their point of view over one another, bullying is more along the lines of one strong-willed person continuously getting harassed by a bully (or bullies).

It should also be remembered that no man (or woman) is an island onto themselves; not only do we need relationships but the quality of a relationship can affect the well-being of even the most esteemed person. And in the relationship between bully and target, the target's levels of overall well-being can certainly receive a very strong knocking. Even if you have one of the highest levels of happiness, esteem, confidence, etc, a bullying if not dealt with can produce a negative grinding effect, chipping away at these attributes till they no longer exist.

One of the main changes in the personality of a person being bullied can be a loss in confidence and self-esteem. What exactly is self-confidence and self-esteem? Unfortunately self-confidence is quite a hard thing to define, if not simply because of the vast number of different interpretations there are. Some definitions see confidence more as an assurance of oneself, other definitions describing it more in line with arrogance. Yet I define self-confidence as *'an assurance, trust in our abilities.'* Fortunately most of the definitions on self-esteem are the same, *'a person's overall evaluation or appraisal of his or her own worth.'*[1]

Research has shown how the effects of bullying on ones self-esteem and confidence can be crushing. Research carried out by psychologist Dr Stephen Joseph on 331 school pupils

---

[1] Quote taken from Wikipedia (self-esteem) URL - http://en.wikipedia.org/wiki/Self-esteem

uncovered that 40% of them were at the time being bullied.[2] Further still, he observed how these students seem to suffer from post-traumatic stress. His research in particular noted how those that were being bullied also displayed far lower levels of esteem compared to those students who weren't.

Although his research was carried out on adolescents, it is pretty much guaranteed that the lowering of esteem and confidence also occurs in adults who being bullied. Ask any competent therapist who has treated a patient who was the target of a bullying (especially that was prolonged) and they would agree that these are common characteristics within such patients.

Unfortunately the lowering of self-esteem and confidence is not the only change in the targets personality. Another change commonly witnessed in one who is being bullied is the increase in one's reactivity. Targets of bullies can at times become very hot-headed and instead of responding to an event calmly (like they might of before) would react to the same stimuli with a burst of anger and/or anxiety. For instance, if a target is been bullied at work, she may become very closed off to her loved ones with regards to how her day at work was and when pressurised about her reticence, might explode in a rage of anger, or will simply burst into tears and walk away.

Many people who knew Henry would know that he certainly enjoyed his job. Being a bit of a self-confessed nerd, he loved working in computer science. While he always had a passion for computers, he particularly loved programming, in particular, the writing of a script for a computer program, followed by running the program and spotting any errors that occur in the script.

Despite being an excellent programmer, Henry was nowhere near as talented in regards to making friends. Like the stereotypical image of a nerd, Henry would speak fast and waffle on when in the presence of others. As such, he generally preferred to spend time on his own. Being a socially awkward person, this perceived weakness became obvious to others, especially to Ed, who in many ways was the opposite of Henry. Ed was socially

---

[2] Dr Joseph research was carried out in 2003 and was published in his paper 'Peer – Victimisation and Posttraumatic Stress in Adolescents'

confident, slightly arrogant even. Yet when it came to programming, Ed was mediocre, compared to Henry anyhow.

Unfortunately this difference in skill led to resentment in Ed towards Henry and instead of taking the higher road, Ed decided to start poking fun at Henry. First it was in subtle ways, the odd joke to mutual acquaintances at Henry's expense. Unfortunately as time went by, the jokes became only one form of attack in Ed's arsenal against Henry. Ed, becoming a Blitzer bully, began developing an audience of fellow immature workers as he began hurling insults and jokes at Henry throughout the day, each comment being followed by laughter and encouragement from certain other members of the office as well.

Naturally the bullying tactics led to a lowering in Henry's overall happiness as his confidence, etc plummeted. On coming home in the evening, his wife noted that he was no longer his usual happy self, instead was moody and reserved. Unfortunately her concerns that something was up soon become realized when on asking Henry what the problem was, he reacted in a very angry manner (something she was not use to from him), telling her to mind her own business. He then stormed off, leaving her standing there shocked at what had just taken place.

A few days later when Henry had seemed to settle down, he and his wife were driving back from the DIY store. As she was driving, she decided to take the route home passing Henry's work, just to observe his reaction as they went past his office. To her horror, as they turned onto the street where his office was, she noted that he began trembling with fear, which increased as they got closer to his work. On becoming level with the front of his office, Henry couldn't seem to hold it in anymore and did something she'd hadn't seen him do for many years, burst into tears like a small child.

Apart from the loss of confidence, esteem and becoming more reactive, another change often witnessed in the personalities of targets is the reduction in their levels of enthusiasm towards the setting (or taking up) of work and general tasks. Instead of being open and creative, pursuing individual or group goals, targets of prolonged bullying can become more withdrawn, tending to do what is needed and not willing to go the extra mile.

This lack of motivation is probably a secondary attribute, brought about due to the lowering of the target's self-esteem and confidence. Studies in psychology, etc have shown a strong correlation between ones self-esteem and one's motivational levels, mainly being that when one is higher, so is the other. It should also be mentioned that along with the reduction in motivation, one's creativity is quashed as well, as in the case of a target, the lack of esteem will very often lead them to believing that ideas of their own aren't good enough to be expressed and so remain just ideas!

In today's competitive age where speed and innovation is the way, every organisation needs to be able to muster the internal resources and motivation of everyone within it in order to survive; whether the organisation be a charity, business or government department (even social organisations need to be able to come up with new social activities in order to keep going). Unfortunately the presence of bullies within an organisation can be like a ball and chain to the running of the organisation. If not dealt with, it could even lead to the death of the organisation (especially if the organisation needs to keep moving in order to survive).

Unfortunately, once a bully is in operation within an organisation, the effects can already be damaging in untold ways, yet naturally the higher up a bully is in an organisation, the more damage they can do. A bully who is vice president or district governor can do far more damage than a bully who is just an account manager or team leader; due to the fact that their standing in the organisation means that they have more power over a greater number of people, hence greater number of targets. Likewise, the higher up they are, the harder it is to take them out (though there are stories of even bullying CEOs being booted out by a board of shareholders who fortunately caught on to their ways and the damaged caused).

Yet how can bullies actually affect the running and success of an organisation? Well the fact that there is a bully in an organisation means that there would also be targets (those unfortunate enough to be on the receiving end of the bullying). As such, these targets are not going to be able to give their best to the organisations they serve; due to greater reactivity levels, lowering of motivation towards a job, etc. In other words, a decrease in both quality and quantity as potential key players don't step up to the mark due to lack of confidence, etc. Likewise, absenteeism is likely to increase due to stress of being bullied.

Also, it is not uncommon of bullies to often take credit for work that their targets did or exaggerate to those higher-up in the organisation on how things really are, let's not forget, bullies are cowards and more often than not, spineless. As such, a bully will often suck up to those he sees higher than himself in the organisation as they could aid him in his own standing or simply make his life easier. Yet this sort of behaviour is damaging to an organisation in that at the very least, it is giving the wrong impression about how things are, and an organisation where its decision-makers don't really know what is really going on can ultimately be doomed to failure.

Another reason why it is not worth having a bully in an organisation is due to the fact that many bullies tend to inadvertently create their own sub-culture, this being especially true with the Blitzer ones who seek an audience of willing participants to join them in their campaign (whether by actively bullying the targets as well or just laughing along and being a general support to the bully).

With such a bully in the organisation, even the most well-intentioned mission statements mentioning the organisations ethos become nothing more than nicely framed statements hanging on the wall. A bully (especially one who has reached a specific level within the organisation) can completely flip the ethos of the company around, sharing ideas and supporting those who are equal or higher up then him, yet using fear and terror on anyone below him who he perceives as weak. With such a bully in place (in particular, a Blitzer) others learn that it is perfectly okay to behave in such a manner to someone weaker than them; and those who are weak within themselves will express such behaviour as well.

In the many different organisations that I have worked in or joined, one personal observation that I have made is that it is the organisations; be it a social, charity or business who don't believe they have bullies within their midst or worse yet, welcome bullies (mistakenly perceiving a bullies aggressive cowardice as a leadership trait) are the ones who have most bullies within them. Ironically, those that have a strict anti-bullying policy tend not to have many bullies within their midst. Though if you are the head of such an organisation, beware, even the odd bully often slips through the net once in a while. Once in, are similar to cockroaches in that it is often hard (and costly) to flush them out!

BULLYING MYTH

It is surprising how many myths there are in regards to bullying ranging from 'All bullies suffer from low self-esteem' to 'bullying only happens in the school yard between children.' In this chapter, we will look closely at these myths amongst others and reveal how they are just that; Myths, probably thought up by well-intentioned people who have unfortunately go it way wrong.

The first myth we will look at is;

Bullying Is Something That Happens In The School Yard

Though this myth is fundamentally wrong, it does contain a small fragment of truth in that bullying is generally more common at school amongst children than adults. Fortunately as children grow up, it appears that many of the bullies who taunted their targets in the playground mature and realise that what they are doing is wrong, uncool, etc.

Unfortunately if this were true for all bullies, than bullying would only occur amongst children and there would be no reason for you to be reading this. Sadly, some people remain bullies as they grow from children into adults, the only difference being that the bully within has had to adapt (I am not aware of circumstances where a non-bully child grows up to become a bullying adult though there is no reason why it can't happen).

The reason why this myth can be harmful is because if believed by a target of a bully, they may refuse to acknowledge that the bullying is happening. It is well known by psychologists, etc that a lot of the time we humans don't see reality as it really is but instead perceive it through a thick pair of distorted glasses called our 'Belief Systems.' For instance, rain is neither good nor bad, it just is. Yet the beliefs we hold about rain affect how we feel when it does rain. I personally love it when it rains (when indoors that is) while many people I know find rain as slightly depressing.

In more extreme way, a belief in the myth that bullies only occupy the schools of the world would probably lead to the target denying the fact that they are being bullied and so simply put up with it.

Bullies Have Low Self-Esteem & So Need Our Compassion

There is a strong conviction amongst many psychiatric and mental groups which states that people who intentionally cause suffering to others must not be happy in themselves for no happy person would willing increase suffering. Therefore, bullies are really people who are deeply unhappy in themselves and as such, need our compassion, not condemnation.

From my experience, there is a large amount of truth in this statement; many bullies are bullies because they themselves are suffering in some way. Such sufferings can stem from issues such as a poor home or work life, (it is not unknown for a bully to be the target of another bully) or personal issues such as low self-esteem, envy, jealously, anger issues.

Either way, if the bullying is simply an expression of some other issue, take note that this does not make the bullying acceptable. We all have problems of one sort or another; I don't believe that anybody lives a charmed life (well not for prolonged periods) yet just because we all have issues, it doesn't mean that we have the right to take our anger, bitterness, etc out on another.

However not all bullies have what one would cause 'issues.' For many bullies, the bullying stems from the fact that they have learnt that by tormenting and intimidation, it can get them what they want quite a lot of the time, as well as having the secondary payoff of giving them a temporary sense of power. *'I can make x or y break down into fear the moment I want, how exhilarating'* is the thought processes of these types of bullies.

Yet whether a bully is picking on you due to certain problems in their own life or whether your bully is just a bully because he gets a payoff from it, you shouldn't be feeling compassion for them, no matter what any do-gooder says. Instead, read on (especially in chapter 6) on how to confront the bully.

Back in 2006, the to-be Prime Minister David Cameron once openly stated that we as a society need to have more compassion towards the 'Hoodies,' young people who tend to

walk around in hooded jumpers, with the hoods up. Though it is wrong to generalise, hoodies very often tend to be criminals and bullies, in that they often pick on hardworking, upstanding citizens of society (like punks used to in the 1970s).

Naturally his speech generated a large amount of mockery from the media, who labelled his speech as 'hug a hoodie.' Thankfully most people can see that such people don't need compassion but a proverbial boot up the backside!

Bullies Come from Poor Or Broken Home & Tend To Be Of Lower Class

Now this myth is so untrue that it deserves to be put in the same category of myths such as 'You can see the Great Wall of China from the moon.' With regards to class, there are bullies on all ends of the class spectrum; from the upper aristocracy all the way down to the working man or woman. Similarly there are also targets on all points of the class spectrum as well. While a bully may pick on a target due to their class, bullying in itself has nothing to do with class.

Now in regards to a 'poor or broken home part' of the myth, bullies don't always come from poor backgrounds or from dysfunctional families. Many bullies actually come from very wealthy families, though one could argue that there must be some form of dysfunction in a family if one were to raise a bully in the process. I personally don't believe this to be the case for there are some people who become bullies not due to a dysfunctional upbringing, but simply because they have caught on that this behaviour can work in their favour.

Yet on saying that, I do believe that there are cases where a bully becomes a bully due to their upbringing. Just like when a boy who sees his father beat up his mother learns that it is acceptable to hit a woman, so a child who sees his parents act like bullies learns that this is the appropriate way to behave.

It Is Just A Personality Conflict

There is a big difference in the relationship between a bully and the target and two people with strong willed personalities caught in a conflict. For one thing, the latter are implied to be of more equal footing in that while either party maybe psychologically hurt from the conflict, both were willing to be part of the conflict, to try and push their views onto the other.

On the other hand, the relationship between a bully and target is completely different. In this type of relationship, the bully is carrying out a campaign of intimidation on the target, with the target either trying to rise above it or trying to retaliate in any way they can, but most often to no avail. The important thing to note is that the target did not ask to enter the relationship but was forced to from the moment the bullying actually started.

So the next time you hear someone saying that bullying is just a personality conflict, realise that these words are coming out of the mouth of either a naïve person or a bully who is probably trying to justify his actions to himself; it isn't so bad when instead of being the bully, you are an equal in a personality conflict. In fact it can be quite nice to know that from that perspective, you have a fighting personality!

Yet nothing could be further from the truth with bullies. Bullies are cowards and the reason why they bully is because they are in control of the relationship. Nearly always, the bully is the attacker in that they are ones who can decide in which interactions with the target they wish to attack, and in which interactions to stay at bay. Yet this isn't the case for the target, they instead take up the defence position. As such, they do not know when the attack will take place or not and as such, are left in a continuous state of fight or flight.

Bullies Prey On The Weak

This is myth is very often said to someone in the form of advice. In other words, toughen up and stop being so weak for bullies prey on the weak (a hidden insult in that advice as well). Yet in reality, nothing could be further from the truth. Bullies don't prey on the weak, but instead on those who they perceive to be weak.

Would you say that Mahatma Gandhi was a weak man? How about King George VI (who led Britain through World War 2) or even Elvis Presley? Well I personally couldn't think of anyone stronger in will, character than these three men. Yet in their lives, all three were bullied; Gandhi by the British who thought they could bully him into submission, King George VI by his father and brother and Presley by fellow classmates when he was growing up.

As you may well recall from what we covered in chapter 1,nearly everyone gets bullied from time to time, the only difference is that those who claim never to have being bullied either don't realise they have or are too insensitive to realise they are being laughed at. Now not everyone in the world is weak, so therefore to say that bullies only pick on the weak is just plain wrong.

Ignore The Bully And It Will Go Away

Unfortunately for me, this is a myth I still find myself falling into from time to time. In the past when I have been bullied, I have often tried to rise above the bullying by ignoring the attempts of the bully or saying a cutting comment back to them when I have the courage. Unfortunately this is just playing into the hands of the bully for they still have control over the relationship, they can choose when to launch one of their attacks at me (thankfully as I am a tall, well-built kind of person, the attacks tend to be verbal rather than physical).

Unfortunately people who are told by others to simply ignore it in the hope that the bully will go away will very often follow this advice, trying to rise above the bullying (taking the incorrectly perceived moral high ground) and as such, won't tackle the problem head on and solve it.

In my experience, this well-intended advice but still a myth is completely wrong, bullies don't get bored when you no longer react and try to ignore them. The reason for this is two-fold. First, thanks to evolution, we humans have evolved to be social creatures, displaying our emotions in all possible ways, if not by the tone of our voice, than by our facial expressions, etc. As such, bullies can often pick up on the fact that even if you are trying to ignore them, they are still getting to you. And let's be honest, they most probably are. I don't believe there is really anyone out there who can sit in a room, have abuse, etc thrown at them and not be bothered by it at all. So don't bother trying to ignore it.

Secondly, remember that by trying to ignore the bully, you are simply giving them the challenge to try harder to get to you. Say a Blitzer bully is throwing insults at you from across the room with an audience watching on in bemusement. You try ignoring them, (remember that everyone can still probably read from your body language that this is upsetting you) so what does the Blitzer try to do? Naturally he does not want to lose the pleasure he is getting so he will probably try harder, saying more harsh comments until you crack. Playing the ignore it game doesn't work.

Aggressive People Don't Get Bullied, So Act Aggressive

This piece of advice is often used in conjunction with the 'Bullies Prey on the Weak.' From my own experience, this isn't at all true. Try walking around in an aggressive manner, or confront the bully with a new, aggressive persona and all that will happen is that the bullying will simply probably change tactic (if it doesn't get physical). Instead of bullying you directly, the bully would deploy other methods to get to you, be it spreading gossip behind your back, using Stealth Attacks or simply becoming a Passive Bully.

Either way, its still bullying; besides which you will lose the respect of others. This is because despite what you may believe, most people don't tend to view out-of-control aggression as strength. Instead, most people perceive people with such aggression as either a challenge (if they are aggressive themselves) or as someone whom they best give a wide berth to. If you want to be seen as the social-outsider (and still get picked on but in a different manner) than this is the approach to take!

Everyone who knows George is aware of his short-temper and his disposition to violence; and he was not at all ashamed of this. As a refuse collector, George was regularly feared by his fellow co-workers who knew that if they confronted him, he would react with swear words and fists. Hence only a few ever picked on him.

Yet in no way was George immune from bullying. Quite the opposite, for when he lost his temper, he would often start spurting his words out and often get them tangled up. As such, others often sniggered about him behind his back. A few brave people started to pick on him; often winding him up as so to get him in trouble with the boss and laugh at the fact that he was sputtering his words out.

Likewise, others would simply act cold to him, taking a quiet dislike to him and laughing at him behind his back but within ear shot of George. Naturally this grounded down on George's confidence, but been a man of pride and image, he simply ignored it, knowing that if he went after all these people, he would very quickly find himself out of a job!

Never Report On A Bully, Nor Seek Help In Any Form

If a bully could have a real best friend, this myth would be it. Bullies literally rely on a target's silence; for the target to believe that to seek out help from someone else is a form of weakness and as such, to fight your own ground alone is a sign of strength. Out of all the myths mentioned, this one is probably by far most prevalent in society. Nobody likes to be perceived as a whistle-blower, a 'grass' who tells.

One of the main reasons why bully's want their targets to feel weak, afraid or ashamed if they tell is so the bully can carry on their campaign with the peace of mind that nobody is going to stand up to them on the targets behalf. Basically, they can carry on doing what they are doing and not get told off.

Yet least of all, it is my opinion that one of a bullies worst fears (except being caught and punished) is that two or more of their targets would meet up and gain support from each other. Let's not forget that bullies are cowards and as such, can happily pick on one target at a time (maybe two or more if they have some help). Yet to pick on three or four people at once (by themselves) is stupid as they know that they will be floored; if not physically than at least verbally. So by having each target as a self-contained individual, one who will not seek out help but react back is what 99% of bullies' desire.

Don't let the bully dictate to you what is right or wrong (obviously based around their own convenience). Stand up to them by seeking out support from other people as well as reporting what is going on to the appropriate channels in your organisation. Also, remember how ironic it is that bullies don't want you seeking out support when certain bullies (mainly the Blitzers, some Manipulators, etc) use their very own support network to bully their targets; this network consisting of those who will join them and laugh at their jokes.

The list of bullying myths mentioned in this chapter are just some of the more common myths targets either believe or are told. The truth is that a myth is just some fact which happens to be untrue. The danger of believing a myth however is that in the process, one may follow this erroneous advice and as such, the bullying will either continue or actually get worse.

Unfortunately there are many more myths out there in relation to bullies, to many to mention in one book. Though do trust your inner gut feeling, when you hear something said to you (even in good faith) that doesn't feel right, trust your gut feeling. One thing I have learnt in my twenty (un-hum) years on this Earth is that nine times out of ten, your gut feeling is right!

MY EXPERIENCE OF BEING BULLIED

The Bullies In My Life

There are many books covering the bookshelves on the subject of bullying and so from this perspective, this book in itself is no different. Yet unlike many of the other books on this subject, what I feel makes this book (especially the next chapter where we cover how to deal with a bully) different from quite a few of these other books is that I like you too have also been the target of a bully. In fact, not one bully, but several bullies throughout various stages of my life; from my schooldays right up to, well even this point in time as I write this (I will admit that the current bullying is being dealt with and the experience in this book has certainly enabled me to deal with it in a superiorly effective, less stressful manner). *Unfortunately while nobody is immune to bullying, you can certainly learn ways of nipping it in the bud, so to speak.*

Now I am not trying to do any disservice to all the other books on bullying by what I'm about to say next (though there are many good ones and I don't want to be sued by every guru on bullying for dissing their book) but many such books lack the personal experience. By this, I mean they are written by people who know all the theories behind bullying and their targets, psychology, etc, but ask such authors if they have personally ever being bullied and they will be hard pressed to come up with a yes. While it is true that everybody gets bullied once in a while, many people are just fortunate enough never to have realised that they have been a bully's target. So to make sure that this book does not fall into the same pile of 'books on the theories of bullying' I will tell you my personal experience of being the target of a bully.

Those who know me will be surprised to learn (probably not actually) that as a child, I was what you would call a slow developer. I didn't start speaking till I was about 3 years old and was also very clumsy as a child, often dropping or knocking things over. So on being taken to a child specialist by my mum, I was told that I have a condition known as Dyspraxia[3] which for those of you who don't know, is a learning disability.

Fortunately at the time of being diagnosed, this condition had being learnt about and systems for children suffering with Dyspraxia had only just been put in place, so I could very quickly be put on a course of physiotherapy and speech therapy (nowadays, most children diagnosed with dyspraxia have to wait a few years from being diagnosed to receiving any form of help due to sheer numbers of such children being diagnosed and limited resources).

Despite the help, my poor co-ordination skills and jumbled up speech (symptoms of dyspraxia) I stood out from my peers in the class. Also being an anxious child didn't really help and so I very quickly became the attention of quite a few bullies. For them, the fact that I had difficulty expressing myself gave them a great source of entertainment; as well being slow in class and generally low in confidence.

Fortunately most of these bullies were verbal bullies and not physical, though I'm not saying that I didn't get caught up in a few fights, especially in secondary school, which unfortunately was an all-boys school and as such, testosterone levels were high. Yet due to help of my older brother and supportive family, I gradually became more confident in myself, my speech patterns became more 'normal' (though those closest to me will say that it has never returned to normal).

Though a few bullies have come and gone throughout my school years, two happen to spring to mind. The first one was a guy called Ali[4] who regularly throughout my primary school years, was a bit of a serial bully, confronting me (verbally and at times, physically)! I had to sort it out by fighting back or telling the teacher, followed by him backing off again. The climax of the bullying came on a week-long school trip to the Isle of Wright, where he made my life a living hell, partly due to the fact that we were forced to share the same room. Thankfully on getting back, I reported it all to the teachers with help of my parents.

The other bully whom springs to mind was a guy called Joe, who I unfortunately came across in the sixth form. Small but mouthy, he used to make my AS classes a living hell, using Blitzer strategies to get a load of others in the class to laugh at his remarks of me. Some of the weaker ones in the class even contributed their own comments about me as well, all

---

[3] For more information on Dyspraxia, what it is, feel free to visit the Dyspraxia Foundation, whose online website is www.dyspraxiafoundation.org.uk
[4] Despite wanting to reveal their names, I have decided it best to alter their real names as to keep their identity hidden

when the teacher was out of the classroom or on the way to the lesson. The odd thing is that years later, one of these weaker people whom I hadn't seen or spoken to in 5 years tried to add me as a friend on Facebook; cheek!

Finally after a few months of continuous attacks and laughter at my expense, I finally had enough and cracked. Looking back, I was not proud of what I did but at the time, I was pushed over the edge. So what did I do? Thinking back, all I remember was hearing what would be his final comment at my expense, then myself marching across the room to him, followed by my right hand round his neck, pinning him against the wall. Fortunately for him (and myself as well) I was dragged away by the rest of the class who seeing what could transpire, stopped me in time.

So what happened afterwards? Well surprisingly, he attended one more class and then just stopped coming, dropping economics as an AS level, despite the plea from the teacher that he was making a big mistake. Thankfully for me, that was the last I ever saw of him but if I could re-do the way I handled the event, I most certainly would. For one thing, I learnt that physical violence isn't the way to handle a bully, and the treatment from classmates who for a while, kept me at arm's length, probably fearing that I was slightly mentally unstable.

For quite a few years afterwards, I didn't seem to be the target of any bullies (well none that I was aware of). Yet this was to unfortunately change when I joined a particular club of a social foundation. Now don't get me wrong, I think that this organisation in question is a fantastic organisation, one of which I am still a member of. Yet on joining this organisation, I unfortunately happened to fall into what I could only call a bad club. On arriving, the club was very cliquey, full of back-stabbing and bitchiness. The ring leaders in this cliquey culture were two girls, one called Diana and the other called Linda.

Diana was very much a Blitzer bully, in that she would verbally throw belittling comments at me, especially on finding out that I was a vegetarian, was happy to voice her opinion over what she thought of us 'vegetables' as she would call us. This even progressed to physical bullying where she would try hit me on back of the head if we had a disagreement. Unfortunately I will confess to having felt a bit tongue tied and not knowing how to handle it, for if a man had hit me in the back of the head (or anywhere else) I would have made sure he would of hesitate to even think doing that again. Yet I'd always believed that a man should never hit a woman. I think that deep down, she knew I wouldn't retaliate and so carried on this bullying campaign towards me.

Linda on the other hand was a Stealth Attacker, one who would continuously make sly and nasty comments towards me. Though not as bad as Diana in the bullying department, she was just as malicious towards me, regularly belittling my personal beliefs as well undermining me in any way she possibly could. I also heard from a few friends I had in the club that she was also spreading rumours and gossip about me, although I never actually heard what this was about me. As a result, many people in the club tended to act cold and aloof towards me.

So why did I not deal with the situation and sort them both out? I hear you ask. Well two reasons really, (actually, excuses more than reasons) one being that as newcomer to the group, I wanted to make a good impression, which I feel these bullies picked up on as a weakness. Yet like many bullies, they weren't nasty to me from day one. Instead it was a slow, gradual process, slowly grinding down my confidence. In fact, my relationship with Diana wasn't always mean; it was peppered with moments of friendliness though these were few and far between.

The other reason for not doing much was because to be honest, I was trying to maintain a friendly attitude, rise above it, and take the perceived moral high ground. Yet finally after a year of being in the club, I decided that enough was enough and so I left this club altogether.

Fortunately a fellow friend of mine who was also facing the same treatment under the hands of both Diana and Linda informed me that instead of leaving the foundation altogether, he'd decided to move to a different club, the (my existing social club) where he regularly updated me on how much kinder people in this club were. After a few months of hearing how well things were going for him, I decided to test the water so to speak and attended a few events within this new club. I can fortunately say that he was not proven wrong.

As I write this, a few years have passed and I can gladly say that I am now the president of my current social club, helping to organise meetings, etc. Unfortunately on becoming president, I discovered that Linda has also being making several strides forward within the foundation and once again, I found myself in the same situation as before. I say this for on finding out that I was the club president, the bullying from her started again. Yet as mentioned, this time I am calm and prepared and am sorting this problem out, using some of the strategies that we will cover in the next chapter.

Before ending this chapter, I would just like to add that on reflection, I feel that one of the reasons I have generally found it difficult to deal with the bullying in the past is due to the feeling of shame that I was the target of a bully. Nobody likes to be bullied and being the target of one can lead one feeling powerless, ashamed, etc. Very often though, these feelings of weakness are amplified when faced with the prospect of reporting the bullying to the appropriate channels or merely seeking support from your friends.

Yet what I am about to say is obviously far easier said than done but '**don't feel ashamed or weak for being bullied.**' Remember, it is the bully who is the coward and should feel ashamed, weak, etc by their actions. Naturally a bully most probably wants you to believe that telling, etc is a sign of weakness simply due to the fact that he can carry on with his campaign of intimidation without getting caught.

Also, the amount of times in my life that I have literally seen a bully break down and run away like a coward the moment they realise that they are either going to get into trouble or have been shown up to be weak. When the control in the relationship shifts from bully to target (sometimes even ever so slightly) it is amazing how quickly the bullying ceases as the perpetrator either retreats or suddenly wants to make peace.

Now tell me who is the weak one; you the target or the bully!

REMEMBER

There is no shame or weakness in gaining external support with regards to bullying, be it from the authorities, therapist or close family or friends.

HOW TO CONFRONT AND BEAT A BULLY

You Didn't Start It, But How You Can End It

No sane person wants to be bullied and would willingly go out of their way to attract a bully. So as a target, don't ever blame yourself for being bullied. Bullying is pretty much always instigated by the bully and directed at the target, whether the campaign be physical, verbal, passive or even a combination of all three. **REMEMBER; YOU ARE NOT ACCOUNTABLE FOR THE BULLYING.** The bullying probably started due to some factor which was beyond your control and was unintentional, such as the way you were sitting or dressed, etc which caused the bully to focus in on you.

Yet as a target, this does not mean there is nothing that can be done to re-address the balance of power within the relationship, or to put it another way, stop the bullying. Many targets (myself included) that have been bullied have been able to confront the problem and deal with it; and in this chapter, I will show you how you can confront or sort out any bully, be it a current bully or any future bully.

Yet before saying what strategies you can deploy to stop the bullying, it is important that we learn how to handle the effects that bullying can have on us. As you may recall in chapter three, bullying isn't just behavioural, in that bullying also has an effect on ones psyche as well; usually a lowering of self-esteem and confidence, heightened state of arousal, etc. These alterations don't only take place when in presence of the bully but tend to overlap into the rest of the targets life as well. For instance, a person who is being bullied at work will most probably also have a reduction of confidence, heightened state of arousal when down the pub with friends, at night in bed, out shopping or in worst case scenario, even on holiday abroad!

Unfortunately when a target is being bullied, one thing which commonly occurs is what psychologists call 'Rumination.' What exactly is this? Well according to Wikipedia, Rumination is;

'...is a way of responding to distress that involves repetitively (and passively) focusing on the symptoms of the distress, and on its possible causes and consequences.'

Or to put it another way, have you ever been kept awake at night due to worrying thoughts about something that happened the day before or might happen during the coming day? This is ruminating in that you are simply replaying what happened (or might happen)in your mind again and again.

Regrettably rumination never seems to actually make you feel better. In fact it always seems to have the opposite effect, leaving you feeling more anxious, stressed and/or depressed! The reason for this is because the human mind is designed to look for the negative, problems, etc in life and as such, each time you mentally go round the situation (i.e. a bullying incident) the more likely you are to emphasize the situation, see it as even worse than it really is.

If you don't believe me about the fact that our minds are naturally pessimistic, than put this book down and for the next ten hours, try and focus on how good your life is and not even think about any of the problems in your life.

How did you do? Well if you are truly honest, I bet that after the initial overview of how good things are in your life, it became a bit of a struggle to keep the negative thoughts out and maintain the Pollyanna attitude to life. So why is the mind so pessimistic? Well no one knows for certain but one theory is that it was an evolutionary trait passed down from our ancestors. For thousands of years when humans were still living in caves, our minds had to quickly learn to spot potential dangers all the time, else we would find ourselves the meal of some hungry predator.

Since then, the man-eating predators have all but gone (especially in the UK) but our minds haven't caught up yet with this change. Therefore when we become the target of a bully, it is not surprising that our minds repetitively rehearse our encounters with the bully, how we should have behaved, then spotting all the problems, potential threats, etc with that solution.

Though your mind might be stuck in a downward spiral, you don't have to be and as science has shown, there are options that you can take to break the mental loop and in the process, completely reverse (if not severely reduce) the psychological effects of the bullying. One such option is the practise of;

MINDFULNESS

The principle of Mindfulness dates back to at least 500 BC, if not even far earlier and in the East, is core to many religious beliefs. Though in recent years, researchers such as Dr Jon Kabat-Zinn have taken the concepts of Mindfulness into the scientific arena, removing the religious elements, leaving the basis of Mindfulness for the masses in both East & West to try.

So what exactly is Mindfulness? Unfortunately there are many different definitions of Mindfulness but the best definition I have heard is;

'...paying attention in a particular way, on purpose, in the present moment and non-judgmentally'

In other words, Mindfulness means to bring your attention out of your chattering mind and into your senses; to focus your attention on whatever is going on around you or within you. For instance,

- What is the temperature around you?
- What can you see around you?
- How does your hand feel?

If you answered the three questions above, then you may have realised that whilst the first two focused your attention onto your external environment, the third question focused your attention into your body, or to be more precise, your hand.

Studies have shown that the practise of Mindfulness has a rather amazing effect on rumination, it weakens it if not completely ceases it. The reason for this is because by taking your attention away from your ruminating mind, the thoughts very quickly subside to a background echo, only popping out briefly when your attention briefly slips back into the mind again. Or if you are lucky, your thoughts completely subside so that when you do finally return to your normal state of being (in ones thinking mind) you'd broken the vicious rumination cycle. As you may have guessed, Mindfulness is nowadays regularly used as a relaxation technique by many throughout the world (including the non-religious).

So how can you use mindfulness to overcome the stresses and ordeal of being bullied? Well if you happen to find yourself ruminating about being bullied, one method you can use to break the cycle is to bring as much attention as you can onto your breathing. Now the trick isn't to actually control your breathing by purposely taking slower, deeper breaths, etc. Instead, just let your attention rest on the fact you are breathing, without trying to control the length or depth of breath.

If like me though, you find that doing the above exercise tricky due to the fact that you are unable to be still long enough to focus on your breath without having something to do, well this next exercise might be more appropriate. Instead of focusing all your attention on breathing, find a relatively simple task to do, say washing the dishes. Yet as you wash the dishes, try bringing all your attention onto the actual process of washing the dishes. Feel what it is like to have your hands in warm, soapy water or the sound the plates make as you stack them up in the dishwasher. Try not to think about the task, instead start to focus on the task at hand, the sights and sounds, etc of doing the above task.

Whether focusing on breathing or performing simple tasks mindfully, you may find your mind trying to pull you back into the rumination cycle again. If this happens and you find yourself ruminating again, just realize what has happened and try again to bring your attention back to exercise at hand. Trust me when I say that after a short while, your mind forgets what it is ruminating over and as you bring your attention back to your mind, the obsessive thoughts have gone!

WRITE IT OUT

One of the problems with rumination is that over time, the mind tends to exaggerate and distort what actually took place. Each time the mind goes over the bullying incident, it seems to alter the facts slightly and usually makes the bullying appear more frightening and difficult than it really was. Hence over a period of time, what you remember as happening could be far worse than what actually happened. As a consequence, this tends to reduce the targets ability to respond to the bullying out of stress and fear, as the memory of the bullying incident becomes worse.

Hence another method to reduce the effects of the bullying is to get the facts straight about what actually happened, not in our minds (as rumination will soon distort those facts) but on paper. So simply grab a pen and piece of paper and first ask yourself the following question

'What actually happened?' Imagine you had just witnessed a crime taking place and were now reporting it to the police. As you were telling him the chain of events within this crime, you would want to be as objective as possible; leaving out as much as possible your own emotional feelings and perspectives for these would affect the details of the police enquiry. Likewise, when answering this question, answer as objectively as you can just listing the events of what happened in regards to the general interactions with your bully.

Next ask the following question

'What is the best solution with regards to this situation?' Now write down a series of possible solutions to the bullying (referring to your previous answer in regards to the type of bullying that is taking place). Also, once you written down a possible solution, write down what would be the possible consequences of that solution. Include potential solutions like physically fighting the bully to reporting it to someone, with the possible consequences behind each solution; physically fighting the bully could lead you to being arrested while reporting could lead the bully to leaving you alone.

Finally when you have a list of solutions, look at which option is the safest and least likely to be damaging to yourself. On finding the best solution, proceed to ask yourself the final question

'What small steps can I take to bring this solution about?' Simply jot down small steps that you can take to get the above solution working. For instance, if the solution is to report it to someone higher up in the organisation, small steps that you can take is to ask yourself who is the best person to report it to, how will you approach that person, etc.

Once you have done the above exercise, the next step is to take action to get what you set out to accomplish, for nothing will get done until you initiate some form of action.

SEEK OUT SUPPORT

There is great truth in the expression 'A problem shared is a problem halved,' and one which a bully would most certainly not want you to know about, let alone how truthful that expression actually is. As a species, we humans are naturally social animals; if we hadn't of been, then our early ancestors would probably have never made it far out of the caves. As well as a mind which looks out for threats and dangers, another gift Mother Nature has also bestowed on us is the willingness to connect with others. Even the most introverted of us still need companionship every once in a while.

Fortunately it is this need for others that enables us to help reduce the bullying, that is if we have the confidence to approach others and let them know that we are the targets of a bully. Obviously I am not referring to approaching the friends of the bully but instead; other people that you can personally trust and that you know have your best intentions at heart. Such a person doesn't have to even be in the same organisation or social circles as the bully, or even know of the bully.

It is a shame that in our macho society, many think that the idea of approaching another with their own vulnerabilities and problems is a major weakness, like throwing the towel in and saying that you can't handle the problems that you are a small person as a result. Yet nothing could be further from the truth; if this were the case, then why do bullies often try and develop their own support networks of people who will join them in laughing at you as well (or very least, not report what is taking place on your behalf). Intentionally or unintentionally, people who stand-by when they see that bullying is taking place are part of the bullies support network.

So why not even out the playing field a bit more by having a team of people (trusted friends, family) who can support you through the bullying incident, advising you when best on how you can actually deal with the bullying. I'm not necessarily saying that you need to rally people to take on the bully with you, they don't even have to know who the bully is; just people who can look out for you and advise you on what to do.

> **REMEMBER**
>
> When seeking out people for support, make sure that they;
>
> 1) Have your best interests at heart
> 2) Are supportive of you
> 3) Not close friends of the bully or general gossipers.

On creating a support network, this will help a long way towards severely reducing any rumination that you may be experiencing (especially on those long sleepless nights) as well as probably speeding up the process of stopping the bullying once and for all.

By using Mindfulness, Writing It Out or Support Networking, you will certainly be heading in the right direction to deal with the bullying as you will be severely reducing the psychological effects that the bullying is having on you. Now it is time we learnt how to actually go about dealing with the bullying head on. Unfortunately various bullies require different methods of defeating them, yet fortunately the following techniques you are about to learn haven't failed me yet!

DEALING WITH A PHYSICAL BULLY

It would be wrong of me to say that a physical bully is worse than a verbal bully but what I can say however is that unlike the other types of bullies, a physical bully can actually put your life in danger; mainly due to the fact that he is physically touching you with potential intent to do harm.

So how does one go about dealing with a physical bully? Well in the UK, physical bullying is against the law and if someone deliberately touches you with the intent of hurting you, this is an assault (as known by the police, courts, etc). Yet an assault doesn't only include directly touching you, even if the bully happens to throw something at you, spit at you, etc, this is also an assault. Any form of action which leads to you being touched with the deliberate intent of harming or offending you falls into this category.

So as a physical bully is basically assaulting you, you have a choice, either fight back, leave it or report it to the highest authority. In regards to fighting back, I wouldn't usually recommend it as you could end up getting hurt or in trouble (though I'll mention shortly how there is an exception to this). Not doing anything is just as bad (if not worse) as it teaches the bully that this form of behaviour is perfectly acceptable, he will get away with it.

The third option which is the one that I would recommend would be to straight away, go and report what has just taken place. If out in the street or a public place, go straight to the police and report what has happened. If the bullying happens to be within the grounds of the organisation (say inside the office of your workplace) then you have a choice, report it to the highest authority within the organisation, i.e. your boss or up line manager. However if you feel the people in charge of your organisation are weak and that nothing is going to get done, then go straight to the police, letting them know what happened and why you are going to them rather than reporting it within the organisation.

As you may recall, I did mention however that although fighting back is not a response that I would recommend, there is a time though when it is applicable; this being if you are in physical danger and cannot walk away. For instance, if you happened to be in a lift when the physical bully launched an attack on you; in such a situation, just standing there and taking it would not be practical.

Yet I must warn you however, UK law is very clear in that whilst you are perfectly entitle to defend yourself, you are to do so with reasonable force. So if a physical bully were to attack you by shoving you or pushing you, breaking his arm in return would not constitute reasonable force. Yet if he was repeatedly punching you or pulled out a knife, then breaking his arm or disabling him some other way as to cease the attacks on you would be acceptable!

One final word of caution, if you do happen to find yourself in the unlikely event of been confronted by a physical bully, with no means of escape and aim to defend yourself using *reasonable force,* then I must emphasise that when the bully looks like he is no longer going to attack you, then stop. The chances are that both you and he will be going to court and you don't want to look like you are the one who overreacted and be perceived as the perpetrator of violence. **Remember, bullies are cowards and in all likeliness, will turn around and blame you for starting the fight when you were just defending yourself!**

VERBAL BULLIES

As you may recall, there are generally three types of verbal bullies, these being Blitzer, Stealth Attacker and Manipulator. Though their styles of bullying may differ, the way to handle verbal bullies is pretty much the same.

Yet before I proceed to say how, I feel that it is very important to add that you should **NEVER EVER** attack a verbal bully. Unlike a physical bully who may deserve a punch in the face, etc, there are unfortunately a few verbal bullies who want you to react aggressively (not saying these bullies want to fight you, just wind you up, i.e. the Manipulators). Unfortunately if you were to physically attack a verbal bully, you could quickly find yourself in trouble.

So how does one deal with a verbal bully? Well the first course of action would be to get yourself some sort of logbook or journal where you can secretly jot down on paper what happened on each event, what was said to you, etc, and why you find what they said offensive. Remember to add the date and time of each entry as well.

From my experience, there are two advantages to keeping a log of the dates and times of when I was being attacked by a verbal bully. The first advantage is that by keeping a log, when it comes to reporting the bully to someone higher in the organisation, you have a series of events listed to back up your claim. This can be beneficial for unfortunately, many verbal bullies have the 'Gift of the Gab' and can almost talk their way out of anything. So when investigating the claim of bullying, a verbal bully might be able to diffuse the situation by cleverly proclaiming his innocence and the fact that the target is just being hypersensitive.

The second advantage with keeping a log of events is that when looking through your events, you can actually tell whether you are being bullied or not. Now I know this may sound a bit silly but there have been times when I have had a verbal bully, particularly the Manipulator type, who even after our unpleasant interactions, has left me wondering whether I am actually the target of a bully or not. The reason for this is because Manipulators tend to have the sneaky ability to say comments which have double-meanings; insulting to the target yet neutral (or positive) to everyone else in ear shot.

Hence by keeping a log of events, I have been able to get an overview of the interactions and get a sense of whether I was the target of a bully.

Yet even after reviewing your entries in your logbook, if you still can't work out whether you are being bullied or not (some Manipulators can be that sneaky) then the second step you can take (this is an optional step) is to confront the bully when alone and tell them directly how you feel about their comments. Many times, some people don't even realise that they are acting like a manipulative bully. Like myself, there are some people who at times can be naturally sarcastic. We don't tend to be so on purpose; it's just the way our minds seem to work at times.

As you may recall in the first chapter, a sarcastic person (like me) would tend to say the odd sarcastic comment to everyone, whilst a bully would have a few targets that they focus all their comments on. So if you can't work out whether you are the target of a bully or just happen to be around someone who is naturally sarcastic, then you could always tell them how you feel; **Don't tell the person however that you are keeping a record of their behaviour,** just in case it really is a verbal bully. If you do, then expect the bully to be taken aback when you implement the next step.

On informing the person how you feel, if the verbal attacks cease, then the chances are that it was an unintentionally sarcastic person. Yet if the comments carry on (perhaps after a short pause where you simply rattled the bully by honestly approaching them) then the chances are that it is a verbal bully.

Now you know for certain that you are the target of a bully, the final step is to approach someone senior within the organisation that you feel you can trust to report the bullying. If possible, on reporting it, show the person you are reporting it to all the entries within your log. By doing so, it will give credence to your case and make it harder for the verbal bully to talk his way out of it!

Hopefully these steps will be enough in itself for you to deal with a verbal bully, but unfortunately we don't live in an ideal world where all organisations are aware of bullying, let alone prepared to do something about it. If you happen to find yourself in such an organisation, then I would recommend booking an appointment with your local Citizens

Advice Bureau (CAB). By seeing your local CAB, they will be able to tell you the legalities on dealing with such a bully if your organisation is unwilling to do something about it.

WHAT ABOUT PASSIVE BULLIES?

Out of all the bullies, passive bullies are the hardest to catch and stop, simply because a passive bully doesn't directly launch an offensive hate campaign on their targets; at least not an obvious one. Instead, a passive bully tends to be someone who will simply be cold towards you for no apparent reason whatsoever, whilst maintaining a certain degree warmth and charm to everybody else.

Hence when it comes to reporting on a passive bully, stating the case being that you are being treated in a cold manner by this person won't really stand up as bullying in the eyes of most authorities and organisations. The reason for this is that we each have individual rights and one of those rights is to choose who we like and who we dislike. Usually when it comes to someone you dislike, the most mature manner would be to simply act cold to them; not to bully them (in a manner more aggressive than the passive bully does).

As it is your right not to be overly friendly to someone you dislike (and vice versa) reporting their manner as a form of bullying would not hold. Unfair this may seem but unfortunately when it comes to dealing with other people, fairness tends to be a luxury. Worse still, as some people are shallow by nature, their dislike of you might not be something you did or said, instead it might simply be how you look and who you are. Perhaps you were in the wrong place at the wrong time.

Though you can't report on somebody for such behaviour, fortunately there is a technique that you could use to get around the problem, this being to simply approach the perpetrator and ask them (in a kind, concerned manner) if you have done something to offend them, explaining you believe they have due to their attitude towards you. One advantage of doing this is it makes the person aware that you know that they are behaving in this manner. Hence if they weren't trying to be bully you in a passive manner, but just weren't aware how they were behaving, well now they know. Furthermore, if after your encounter, the cold manner still continues, then you'd know that either they are insensitive or they are a passive bully. Either way, the problem lies solely in their laps.

Fortunately this is about as far as a bully can go without being reported. If however you find out that the person in question is spreading rumours about you behind your back or in regards to a working situation, piling you with more work than most others and giving you least praise in return, then there is something that can be done (such bullying unfortunately is occurring in work-based organisations all over the country).

So how can you confront a passive bully and cease their insidious campaign against you? Well the first step would be to approach the bully and confront them about their own behaviour, not in a harsh or condemning way but instead in a more concerned, assertive manner.

Assuming that you have done this initially, with the bully promising that there is no problem and saying he will keep an eye on his behaviour (a common false promise from such people), if the overworking/no praise continues, then I would recommend getting a logbook where you can log every time he overloads you with additional work and not your colleagues, and/or gives you little or no praise on you completing the tasks (perhaps he is even critical of your efforts, despite the work being of a high quality).

Having a series of entries recording his behaviour and why you constitute this as bullying the final step would be to launch an official complaint to someone of a senior position within your organisation who is trustworthy and can look into this situation and get it resolved. Though it may not seem like it is worth complaining about, passive bullying is still bullying and as such, should be dealt with just like the other types of bullying. Why should you have to put up with having your views regularly dismissed in group meetings and having more work than most?

If nothing happens after you initially launched your complaint (except the continuation of the bullying), then I would recommend speaking to your local CAB (Citizens Advice Bureau) who can advise you on the best way to legally take this forwards.

WHAT TO DO IF THE BULLY IS THE GUY AT THE TOP

So far we have assumed that within the organisation where the bully operates (be it an office, charity or social group) the bully is someone who is either at the same level as yourself or only slightly higher up then you in the organisation. Yet what about the rare nightmare scenario, where the bully is the guy at the top, the chief, number one? Though it may be hard to imagine, quite a few organisations (not necessarily big ones) are founded or run by a bully. Just because a person happens to be a bully, doesn't mean he can't found high up in an organisation as well and be your boss (life can be harsh)!

In the UK, a large percentage of the private sector is made up of small to medium enterprises; companies which have 2-200 employees. So if the bully in question is the guy at the top, reporting your issues to the HR department or directly to him isn't really going to help. In fact, it might have the opposite effect of making you an even bigger target with the threat that any resistance on your part would lead to termination of your employment.

Likewise, a charity that you are actively involved in or a social group could also be founded or run by the bully, in which case attempting to report the bully would most probably fall on deaf ears. As with the bully CEO, complaining like you would if the bully held a lower position in the organisation would not work.

In this unfortunate circumstance, what can you do? Well fortunately it may be tough but one thing you are not is powerless. Assuming from now on that the bully is the person at the top of the organisation (which happens to be your job), if he was a passive bully or a certain type of verbal bully, you could always talk to them by themselves, telling them that you feel hurt by the way they are treating you and if you had done something to offend them. Please note that if the person at the top is a Blitzer however or a physical bully, than do not approach them. If he were a Blitzer, you can almost be sure that he will be laughing at you later on for approaching him to begin with; and if he is a physical bully, just pack your bags and leave the organisation whatever it may be, work, social, etc, not forgetting to call the police afterwards. Your health and safety is what comes first!

If you approached the bully (or in the case of a Blitzer, didn't) and nothing has changed, then I would recommend that you place your CV online or at recruitment agencies, letting the market know that you are looking for work. If confronting the bully didn't work (or in the case of a Blitzer) the bullying isn't likely going to stop, only get worse as the bully pushes the boundaries and realises more he can get away with.

In the meantime whilst looking for a new job, see if you can't develop a small support network of trusted friends within your working environment; people who you can confide in and potentially may have stories of their own. Knowing that there are people in the organisation who care for your well-being and perhaps going through the same as yourself can be deeply comforting for what can only be described as a very hard time.

In the meantime, it is worth speaking to your local CAB who will be able to guide you through the delicate legalities of having a bully who is your ultimate boss. Current law (and for the foreseeable future) dictates that you can bring your bully boss and his organisation to court where if you are lucky, you might win some compensation for your ordeal. Yet logically, I would only recommend doing this once you have left your job; don't take the Friday off work to take your boss to court and expect to return to work on Monday without any repercussions!

With regards to a social or charitable organisation that you may be involved in, as it is not where you are making your living but simply where you spend your spare time, you have a bit more choice available to you. Yet I would recommend that with as many friends as possible, (or even if just by yourself) quit attending the organisation and go find a better organisation, run by more mature, stronger people. Unfortunately organisations do tend to reflect the personality of the guy at the top and if he happens to be a bully, expect the culture within the organisation to be toxic, especially to your esteem and well-being. As you are not the person at the top with the ultimate say, you won't be able to fight the bully or the toxic culture he has put in place.

So just walk away with your head held high and your sense of worth intact!

CONCLUSION

In our short journey together within this book, we have uncovered how there isn't a particular stereotypical image of a bully. Instead bullies tend to come in all shapes and sizes, from the big guy who uses physical intimidation to the bitchy, condescending female who uses sarcastic comments to get what she wants, as well all those in between these two extremes. We have also uncovered how there is a type of bully whom at first glance is hard to spot as being a bully and once discovered, can be even harder to stop; The Passive Bully.

Fortunately, we have also learnt how no matter whom the bully is (what position in the organisation he holds) as well as the type of bullying; you are not powerless in being able to stop him. Like the rest of us, bullies are only humans though unlike most of us, bullies generally are emotionally stunted humans in that they have some problems within themselves that causes them to seek temporary pleasure by targeting their anger, misery, etc onto somebody else. The targets which they choose to gain a sense of pleasure from tend to be the ones whom they perceive to be weaker than them and so will probably not put up enough of a challenge to stop them. This is one of the reasons why bullies are cowards for they tend not to target those who they believe will physically or emotionally crush them in return.

Having said that, I am by no means implying that the target of a bully is in anyway weak, just perceived as weak by the bully. For instance, a quiet person who doesn't argue or gossip about others may well be perceived as weak from the perspective of the bully, though unbeknownst to the perpetrator, the target has very high IQ and is quiet mostly due to him being a good listener, still high in confidence. Or even better, the quiet, non-aggressive target may actually hold a black belt in karate, which may very quickly leave the bully living to regret his initial judgement.

A few years ago, a rather comical incident was mentioned in the news, about two trouble-making physical bullies were out intimidating people on a Saturday night in the streets of London. Anyhow it just so happens that whilst out (and in front of the CCTV cameras) they spotted two other guys dressed in woman's clothing, later revealed to be on their way to a fancy dress party.

Anyhow both the yobbish bullies decided to run up to these two guys and start a fight with them. Yet unbeknown to the bullies, their intended targets were not just ordinary people but highly trained CAGE FIGHTERS! Anyhow, the incident resulted in one of the bullies getting his head smashed into the pavement (literally) whilst the other was punched to the ground. In front of cheering onlookers and getting up dazed with a bloody nose and in a haze, the bully punched to the ground got back to his feet, took a few steps away from his target (leaving his friend behind) and walked into a lamppost, falling to the ground again! Bet they won't be doing that again in a hurry.

Though the above incident is an extreme rarity of bullies getting their just-desserts, you don't have to be a cage fighter or black belt in any martial art in order to stop a bully. As you may recall, I would strongly recommend not using any violence on a bully but seek out support from another, preferably someone in authority. Yet if you feel that your life is in danger (if you confronted with a physical bully) than by all means do fight back but with what the law describes as *'appropriate force.'* Any other circumstances where you initiate the first move in a fight can lead you to get into trouble with the police (and as bullies are generally emotionally stunted people, I don't really see your bully suddenly developing a sense responsibility and confessing that it was really his fault).

Fortunately we have also uncovered several different non-violent strategies that you can apply in order to stop the bully's hate-campaign against you. We learnt how despite there being several different types of bullying styles, there are non-violent strategies that you can use in order to stop the bullies hate campaign being directed at you. Though very few (if any) bullies actually use justly one of these (most use bits of each style) we uncovered these styles to be;

Physical Bully

Verbal Bully

- Blitzer
- Stealth Attacker
- Manipulator

Passive Bully

Though the bullying styles vary quite somewhat, the strategies that you can use to stop the bullying mostly tend to be based around the idea of reporting the bullying to someone else higher in the organisation, whom you believe has the authority and trust to get the problem sorted. Fortunately if there is no one higher up in the organisation then the bully, you can still report the problem to the Citizens Advice Bureau (CAB) who will be able to direct you on legalities and what you can actually do.

As well as the strategies that can be used to stop the bullying, we also looked at some techniques that you can apply to reduce the effects that bullying has on you. No man or woman is an island; we are naturally social animals and as such, are affected by each other on various levels. Hence even though we might try and deny it, bullying will naturally have an effect on ones psyche and well-being. From my own experience, I even believe that if you consciously try and deny that you are been bullied, the affects to your sense of self will actually be more damaging rather than less.

We came across three different techniques that you can use heal yourself from the bully, these being

Mindfulness – Learning to accept what has happened in the past and bringing your attention back into the present moment, living life non-judgementally. This can be crucial in helping our over-anxious minds to calm down.

Support Network – How having a network of trusted friends (not necessarily in the same organisation as the bully) can also be of great benefit. There is truth in the saying 'a problem shared is a problem halved.'

Writing It Out – We also learnt that writing about the bullying, what is taking place; etc on paper is good in that it helps focus our overactive mind and come up with a solution to handle the bully, healing one's psyche and well-being in the process.

As well as how to heal one's well-being, we also looked at some of the myths on bullying which unfortunately are still prevalent within society. Very often, someone seeking help against bullying will actually be unintentionally informed of one these myths under the disguise of good advice. Such myths which may be erroneously given include 'Bullies have low self-esteem and so need our compassion' to the simple 'Bullying only happens in the playground.' Such myths, if believed by the target, can almost be as destructive as fear in the process of getting the bullying stopped. In an ideal world, one should be able to report on a bully whenever necessarily (even if the bully isn't targeting them but someone else).

Though no one is truly immune to the effects of bullying (even someone with a black belt in martial arts, though the bullies that do pick on such a person are most likely not going to be the physical type) each one of us has the power and ability to stop a bully in their tracks. Bullies are after all emotionally stunted people and as you are hopefully emotionally developed, you have the resources within you to deal with the bully. Hopefully in the reading of 'Beat The Bully: A Guide To Dealing With Adult Bullies' you'd now come to realise the best way to use those resources!

On a final note, if you are contemplating whether or not to take action to stop a bully, (whether the target be yourself or someone else) please remember the expression **'Evil prevails when good people stand by and do nothing.'** As a bully most probably has several different targets on the go at any one time, just one target standing up to the bully can cause the bully to stop his intimidation campaigns and as such, free up all the other targets!

KEEP IN TOUCH

If you have enjoyed reading this book and would like to keep up to date about bullying, than why not subscribe to the companion site to this book, www.beat-the-bully-book.com where you can subscribe to our bi-monthly e-newsletter, sent straight to your e-mail account. There is no paying for this service and you e-mail details are kept confidential from any 3rd parties.

As well subscribe to our bi-monthly newsletter, you can also read relevant news posts on what is taking place around within the sad world of adult bullying. So if you'd like to keep in touch, feel free to visit www.beat-the-bully-book.com

Lightning Source UK Ltd.
Milton Keynes UK
UKOW04f1911230615

254012UK00001B/88/P